AF407566

Draw a Picture

I Can...

- [ ] use a Capital Letter
  The cat is big.
- [ ] use spaces
- [ ] sound out words
  d-o-g = dog
- [ ] use a Period .
- [ ] Draw a picture

He is having fun, running under the sun with his new toy gun.

fun	gun	run	sun
distracţie	armă	alerga	soare

Name: ____________________ Date: ____________________

Today is: Monday | Tuesday | Wednesday | Thursday | Friday

Direction: Trace and read the sentences.

bag	rag	tag	wag

sac	cârpă	etichetă	datul

He has many bags.

I see a rag.

I see a tag.

Its tail is wagging.

My Sight Word List

English - Romanian

a	in	said
and	is	see
away	it	the
big	jump	three
blue	little	to
can	look	two
come	make	up
down	me	we
find	my	where
for	not	yellow
funny	one	you
go	day	
help	play	
here	red	
I	run	

Name: ____________________ Date: ____________________

Today is: Monday Tuesday Wednesday Thursday Friday

Direction: Trace and read the sentences.

fun	gun	run	sun
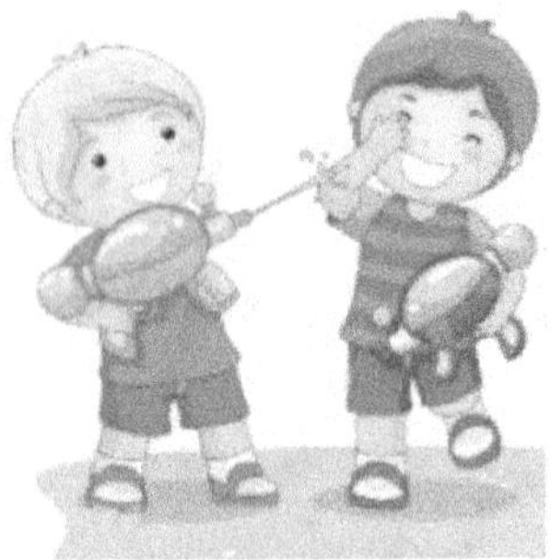	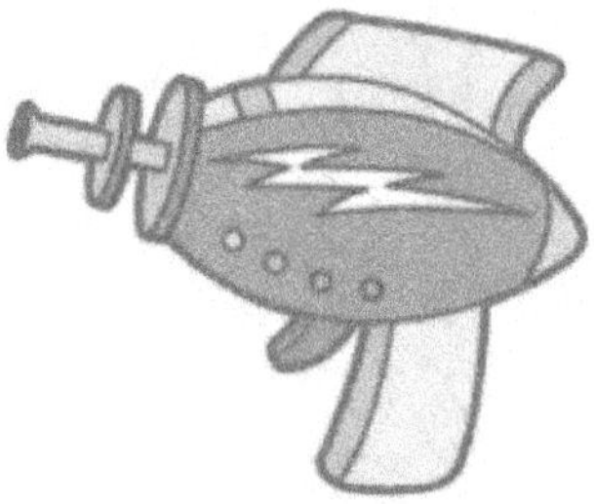	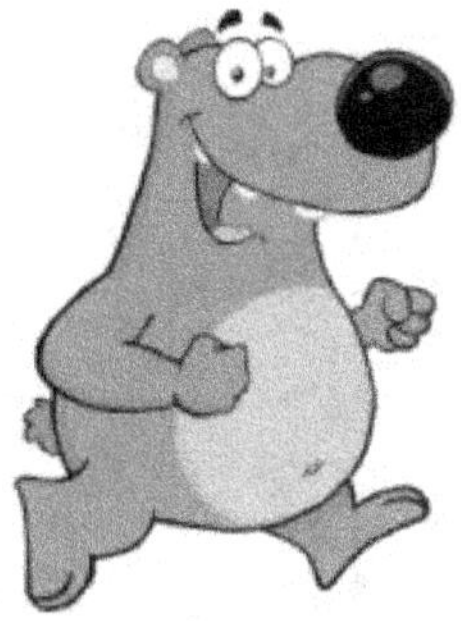	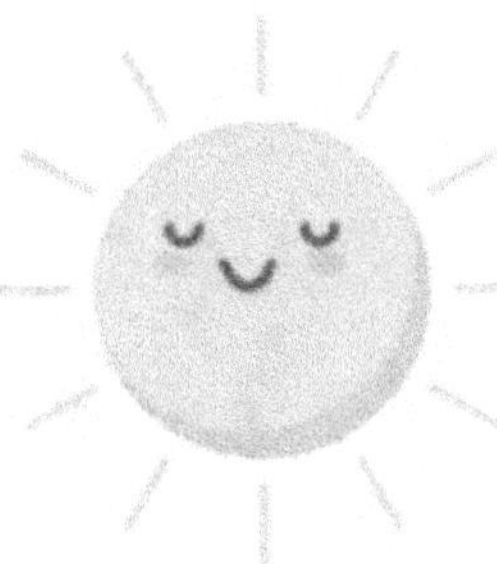
distracţie	armă	alerga	soare

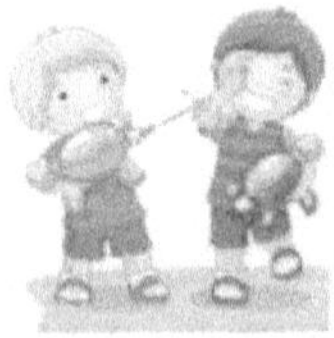

They are having fun.

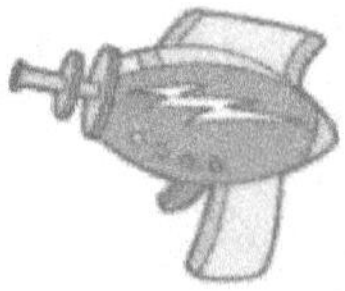

He has a gun.

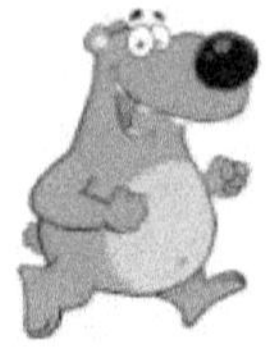

The bear is running.

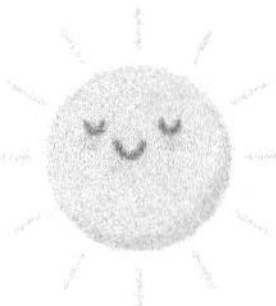

The sun is smiling.

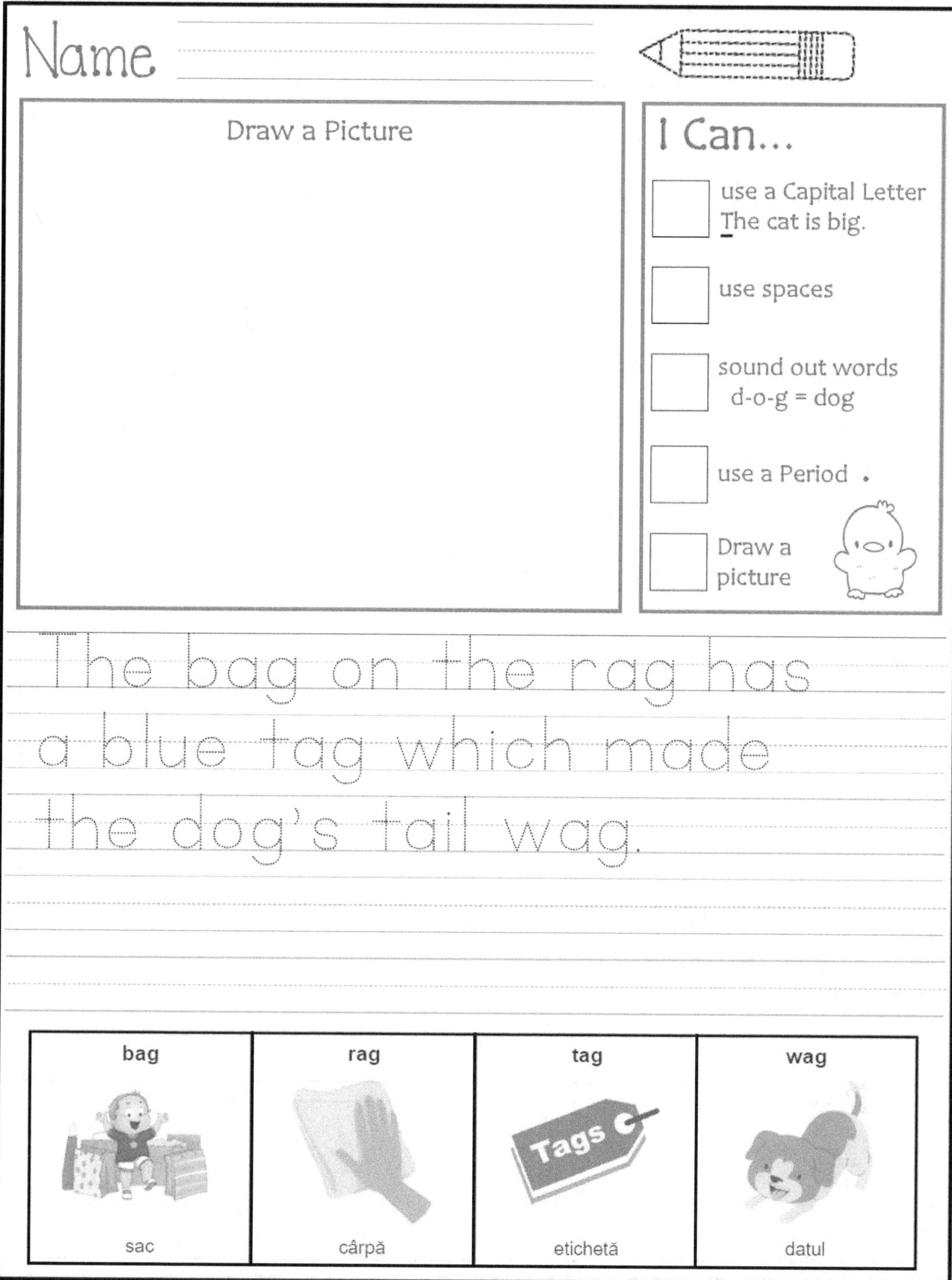

The bag on the rag has a blue tag which made the dog's tail wag.

Name: _______________________ Date: _______________

Today is: [Monday] [Tuesday] [Wednesday]
[Thursday] [Friday]

Direction: Trace and read the sentences.

can	man	pan	van
o cutie	om	tigaie	dubă

I see a can of soda.

The man is happy.

The pan is dirty.

I see a big van.

The man who was driving a van ran over a can and a pan.

can	man	pan	van
o cutie	om	tigaie	dubă

Name: ______________________ Date: ______________________

Today is: Monday Tuesday Wednesday Thursday Friday

Direction: Trace and read the sentences.

cut	gut	hut	nut

tăia	intestin	colibă	nuca

He cut his nails.

He has a gut.

This is a small hut.

It is holding a nut.

Draw a Picture

I Can...

- [ ] use a Capital Letter
  The cat is big.
- [ ] use spaces
- [ ] sound out words
  d-o-g = dog
- [ ] use a Period .
- [ ] Draw a picture

A boy swallowed a nut and
it got stuck in his belly.
He had to get his gut
cut open in the hut.

cut	gut	hut	nut
tăia	intestin	colibă	nuca

Name: ___________________ Date: ___________

Today is: Monday | Tuesday | Wednesday | Thursday | Friday

Direction: Trace and read the sentences.

fat	cat	hat	mat
gras	pisică	pălărie	mat

I see a fat dog.

This is my little cat.

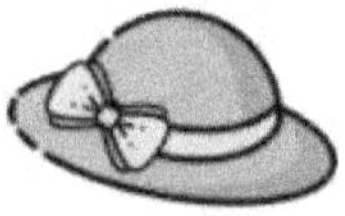

I like this hat.

I see a big mat.

Draw a Picture

I Can...

- [ ] use a Capital Letter
  The cat is big.
- [ ] use spaces
- [ ] sound out words
  d-o-g = dog
- [ ] use a Period .
- [ ] Draw a picture

The fat cat laid on the mat that was a hat pattern.

fat	cat	hat	mat
gras	pisică	pălărie	mat

Name: _________________ Date: _______________

Today is: [Monday] [Tuesday] [Wednesday]
[Thursday] [Friday]

Direction: Trace and read the sentences.

cab	lab	tab	crab
taxi	laborator	fila	crab

The cab is fast.

The lab is exciting.

The tab is long.

We found a crab.

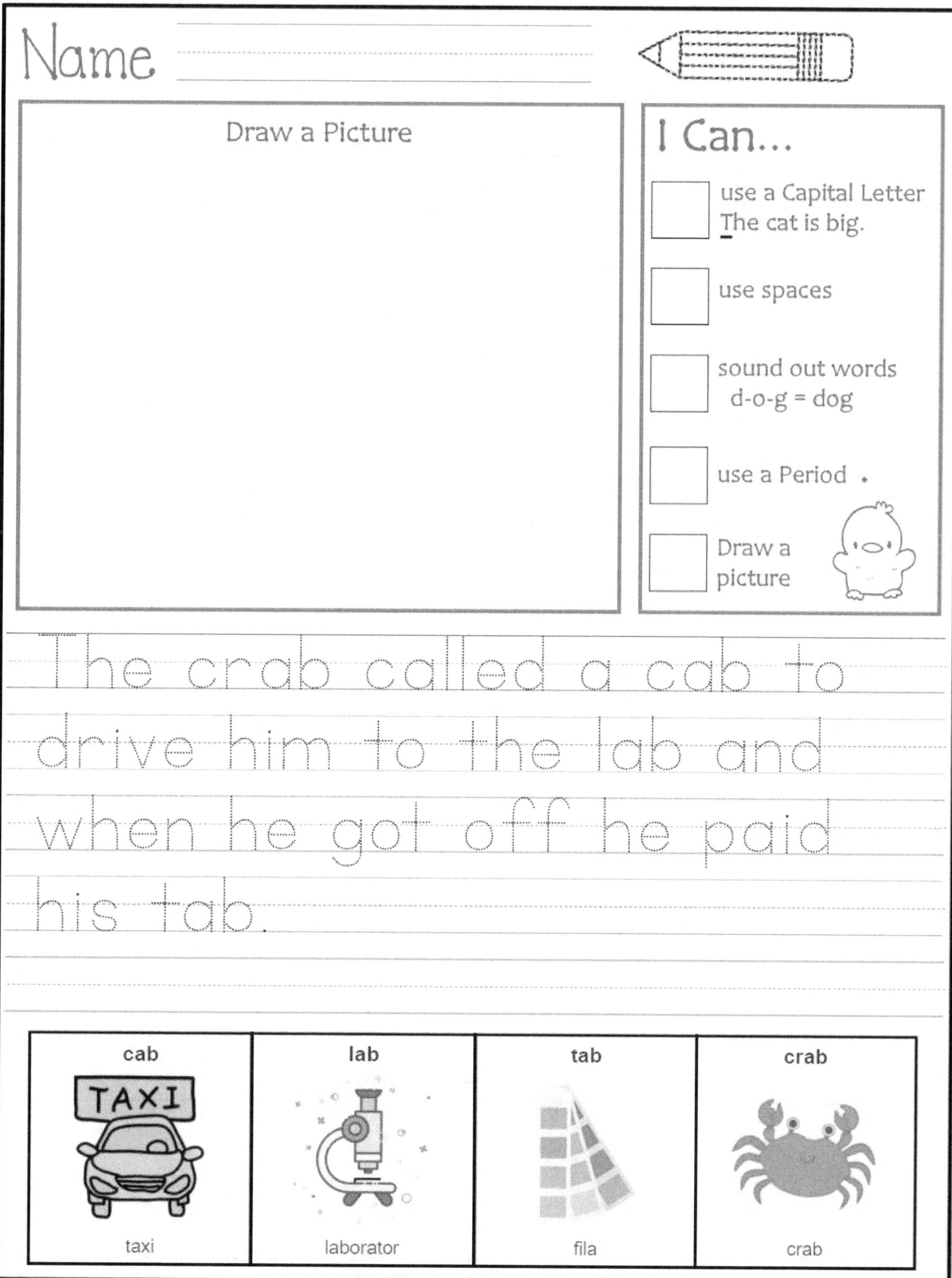

Name

Draw a Picture

I Can...

use a Capital Letter
The cat is big.

use spaces

sound out words
d-o-g = dog

use a Period .

Draw a
picture

The crab called a cab to
drive him to the lab and
when he got off he paid
his tab.

cab
TAXI
taxi

lab
laborator

tab
fila

crab
crab

Name: ______________________ Date: ______________________

Today is: Monday Tuesday Wednesday Thursday Friday

Direction: Trace and read the sentences.

ham	jam	ram	clam

șuncă	gem	oaie	coajă

 I like to eat ham.

 We like to eat jam.

 The ram is big.

 The clam is pretty.

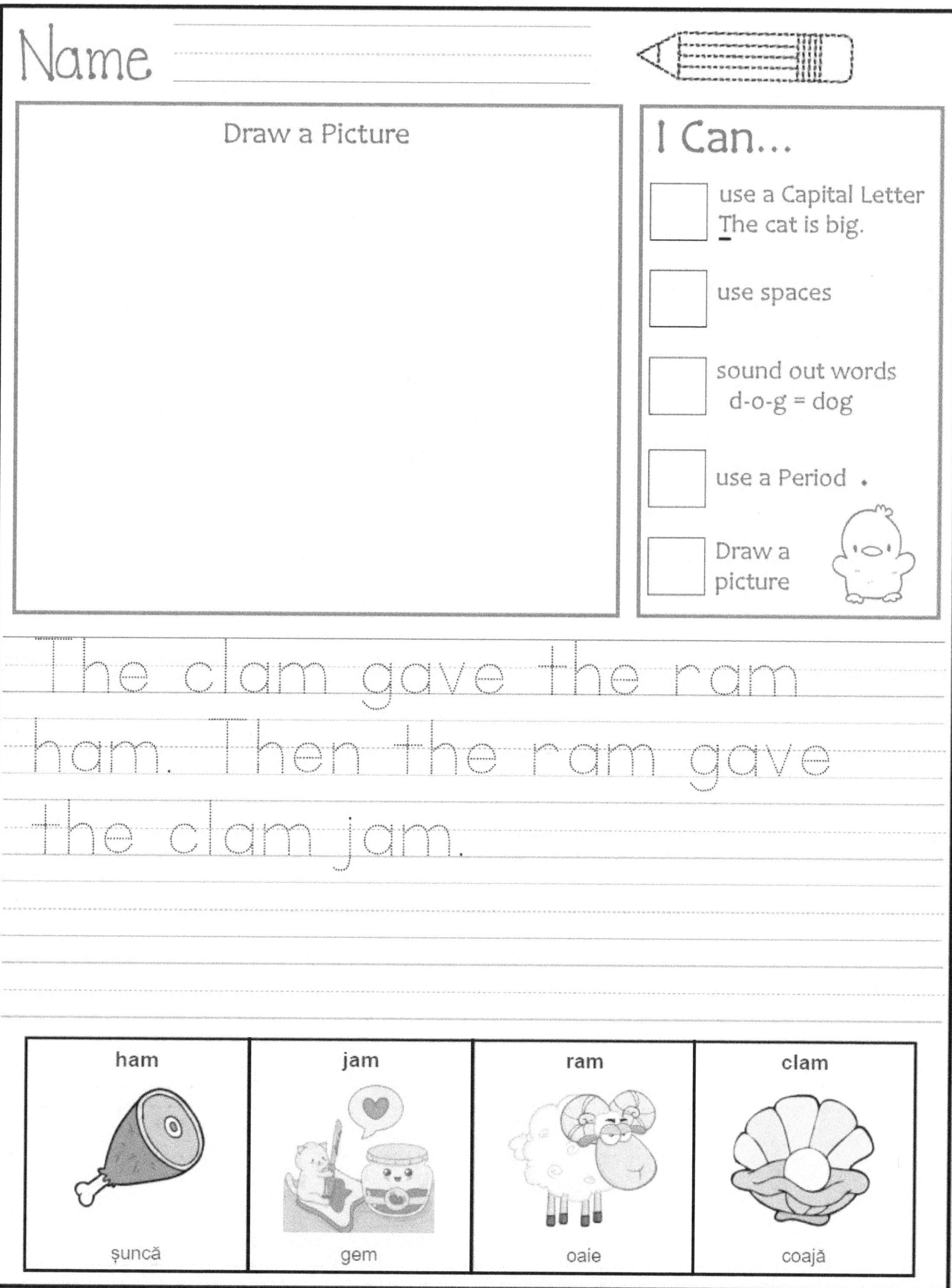

Name

Draw a Picture

I Can...

use a Capital Letter
The cat is big.

use spaces

sound out words
d-o-g = dog

use a Period .

Draw a
picture

The clam gave the ram
ham. Then the ram gave
the clam jam.

ham
șuncă

jam
gem

ram
oaie

clam
coajă

Name: _________________ Date: _______________

Today is: [Monday] [Tuesday] [Wednesday]
[Thursday] [Friday]

Direction: Trace and read the sentences.

| **bed** | **led** | **red** | **wed** |
| pat | conducere | roşu | nuntă |

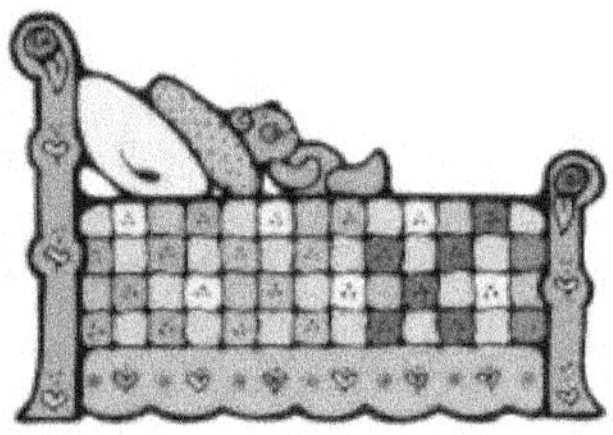

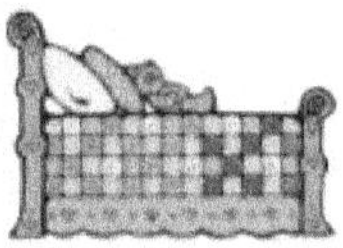

This is my little bed.

He led us to safety.

The apple is red.

He asks her to wed.

Draw a Picture

When the prince got out of bed, he was led on a red carpet to be wed with the princess.

bed	**led**	**red**	**wed**
pat	conducere	roșu	nuntă

Name: _______________ Date: _______________

Today is: Monday   Tuesday   Wednesday
           Thursday   Friday

Direction: Trace and read the sentences.

bad
răa
dad
tata
mad
nebun
sad
trist

This apple is bad.

My dad is very kind.

The reindeer is mad.

The little cat is sad.

I was bad so my dad
got mad and now
I am so sad.

bad	dad	mad	sad
ră700	tata	nebun	trist

Name: ______________________ Date: ______________________

Today is: Monday Tuesday Wednesday Thursday Friday

Direction: Trace and read the sentences.

den	hen	pen	ten

bârlog	găină	grajduri	zece

It is a den.

The hens lay eggs.

She has a good pen.

The ten is smiling.

Name

Draw a Picture

I Can...

use a Capital Letter
The cat is big.

use spaces

sound out words
d-o-g = dog

use a Period .

Draw a
picture

The hen that lived in the
pen laid ten eggs
in her den.

den
bârlog

hen
găină

pen
grajduri

ten
zece

Name: ____________________ Date: ____________________

Today is: Monday Tuesday Wednesday Thursday Friday

Direction: Trace and read the sentences.

gum	mum	sum	drum

cleios	mămică	sumă	tobă

I like to chew gum.

My mum is kind!

I can do a sum!

The drum is big.

Name ______________________________

<table>
<tr><td>

Draw a Picture

</td><td>

I Can...

☐ use a Capital Letter
The cat is big.

☐ use spaces

☐ sound out words
d-o-g = dog

☐ use a Period .

☐ Draw a picture

</td></tr>
</table>

Mum was chewing gum while figuring out the sum of the drum's price.

gum	mum	sum	drum
cleios	mămică	sumă	tobă

Name: _________________ Date: _______________

Today is: [Monday] [Tuesday] [Wednesday]
[Thursday] [Friday]

Direction: Trace and read the sentences.

bid	**hid**	**kid**	**lid**
ofertă	ascunde	copil	capac

He likes to bid.

He is hiding.

The kid like to play.

I see a lid.

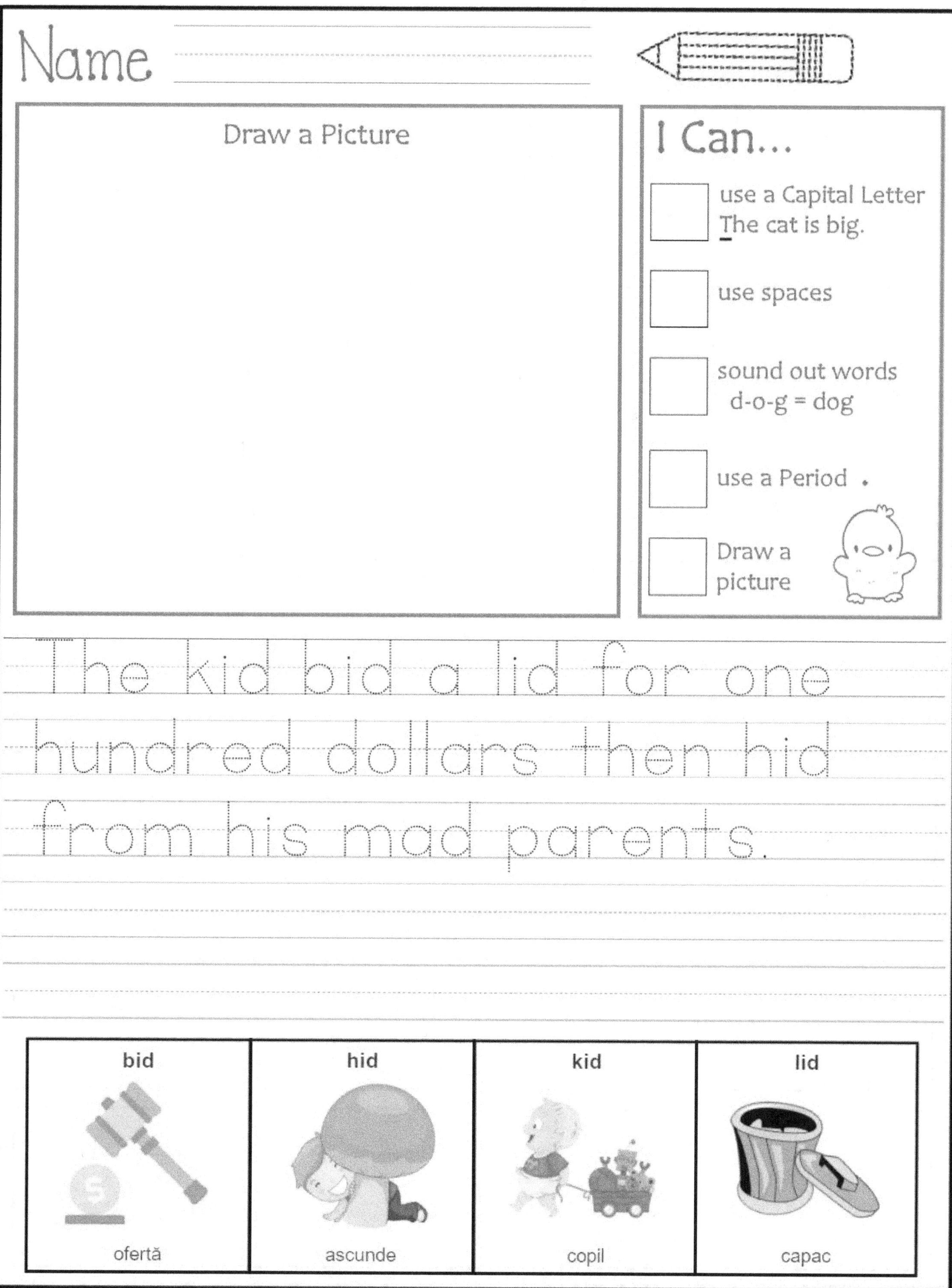

Name

Draw a Picture

I Can...

☐ use a Capital Letter
<u>T</u>he cat is big.

☐ use spaces

☐ sound out words
d-o-g = dog

☐ use a Period .

☐ Draw a picture

The kid bid a lid for one hundred dollars then hid from his mad parents.

bid	hid	kid	lid
ofertă	ascunde	copil	capac

Name: ____________________ Date: ____________________

Today is: Monday Tuesday Wednesday Thursday Friday

Direction: Trace and read the sentences.

big	dig	pig	wig

mare	săpa	porc	perucă

That is a big pencil.

He will dig up a hole.

The pig is fat.

She puts on a wig.

Draw a Picture

I Can...

- [ ] use a Capital Letter
  The cat is big.

- [ ] use spaces

- [ ] sound out words
  d-o-g = dog

- [ ] use a Period .

- [ ] Draw a picture

The big pig went to dig in the mud for his wig.

big	dig	pig	wig
mare	săpa	porc	perucă

Name: _________________ Date: _______________

Today is: [Monday] [Tuesday] [Wednesday]
[Thursday] [Friday]

Direction: Trace and read the sentences.

bin	fin	pin	win
cos	aripioară	bolț	victorie

It is a recycle bin.

The shark has a fin.

The pin is pointy.

He won the match.

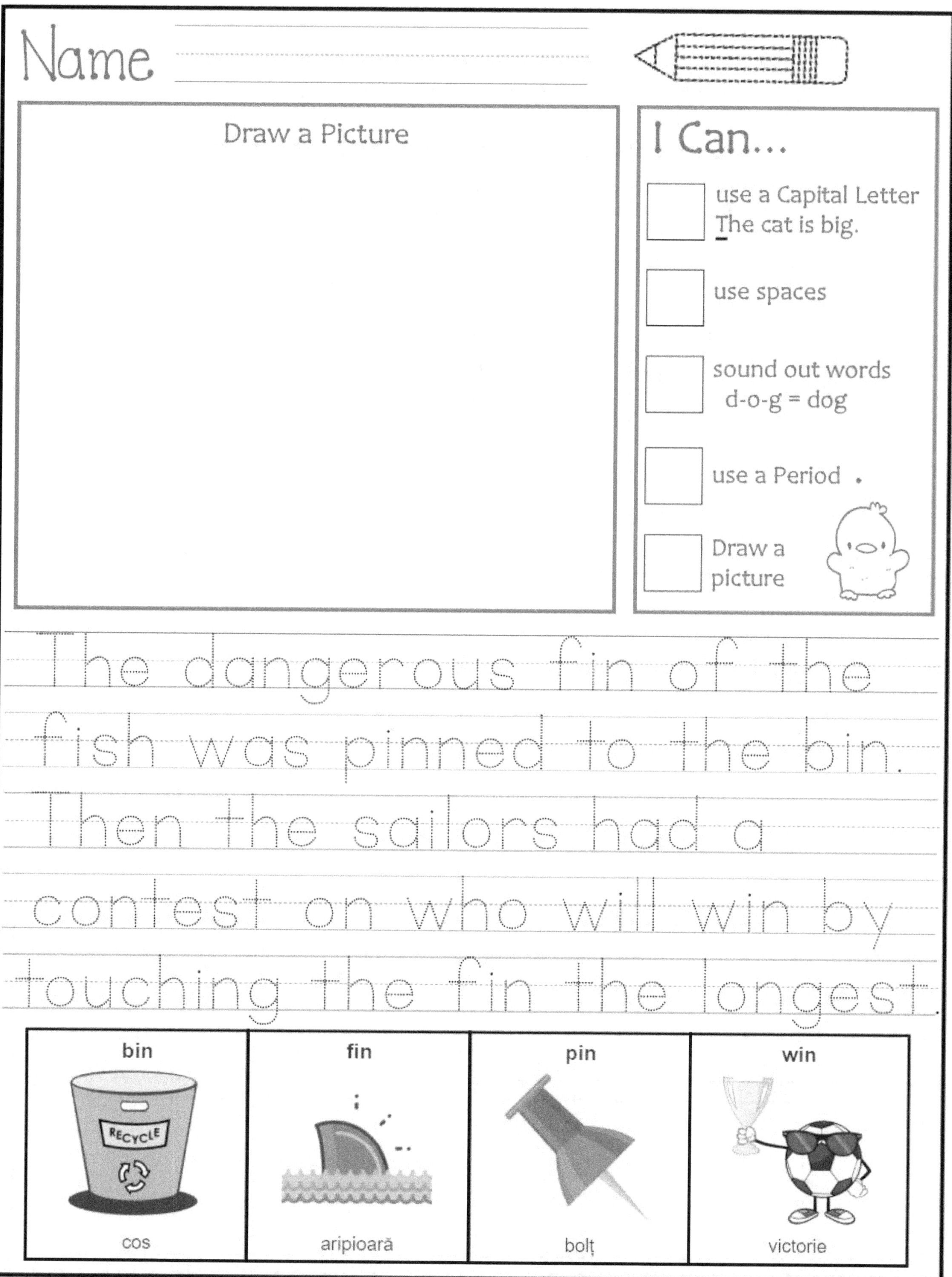

Name

Draw a Picture

I Can...

- [ ] use a Capital Letter
  The cat is big.

- [ ] use spaces

- [ ] sound out words
  d-o-g = dog

- [ ] use a Period .

- [ ] Draw a picture

The dangerous fin of the fish was pinned to the bin. Then the sailors had a contest on who will win by touching the fin the longest.

bin	fin	pin	win
cos	aripioară	bolț	victorie

Name: ___________________ Date: ___________________

Today is: [Monday] [Tuesday] [Wednesday]
[Thursday] [Friday]

Direction: Trace and read the sentences.

hip	**lip**	**nip**	**sip**
șold	buze	mușcătură	băutură

This is my hip.

Her lips are red.

It is nipping its toy.

She is sipping.

Draw a Picture

I Can...

- [ ] use a Capital Letter
  The cat is big.
- [ ] use spaces
- [ ] sound out words
  d-o-g = dog
- [ ] use a Period .
- [ ] Draw a picture

The dog nipped someone who was sipping water with his lip.

hip	lip	nip	sip
şold	buze	muşcătură	băutură

Name: _________________ Date: _____________

Today is: [Monday] [Tuesday] [Wednesday]
[Thursday] [Friday]

Direction: Trace and read the sentences.

fit	hit	kit	sit
potrivi	lovit	trusă	sta

It is perfectly fit.

They hit each other.

That is a safety kit.

He is sitting.

Draw a Picture

I Can...

- ☐ use a Capital Letter
  <u>T</u>he cat is big.

- ☐ use spaces

- ☐ sound out words
  d-o-g = dog

- ☐ use a Period .

- ☐ Draw a picture

The fit doctor sat then was hit by a kit.

fit	hit	kit	sit
potrivi	lovit	trusă	sta

Name: _________________________ Date: _________________________

Today is: [Monday] [Tuesday] [Wednesday]
[Thursday] [Friday]

Direction: Trace and read the sentences.

cob	job	rob	sob
porumb	datorie	jefui	strigăt

I ate corn on the cob

This is my job.

He is robbing.

The girl is sobbing.

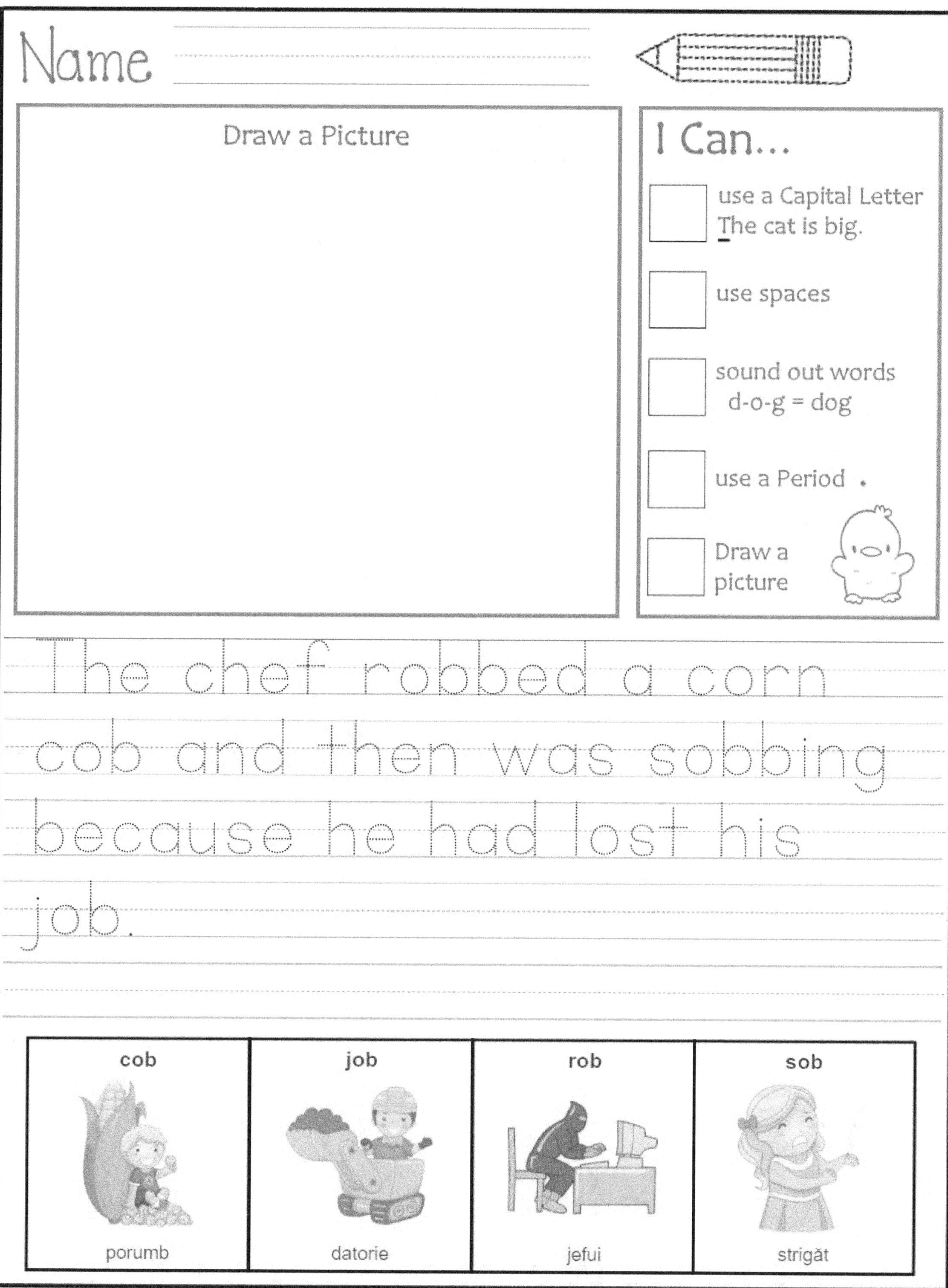

Name

Draw a Picture

I Can...

use a Capital Letter
The cat is big.

use spaces

sound out words
d-o-g = dog

use a Period .

Draw a
picture

The chef robbed a corn
cob and then was sobbing
because he had lost his
job.

cob
porumb

job
datorie

rob
jefui

sob
strigăt

Name: _________________ Date: _______________

Today is: Monday   Tuesday   Wednesday

Thursday   Friday

Direction: Trace and read the sentences.

dog	hog	jog	log
câine	porc	jogging	lemn

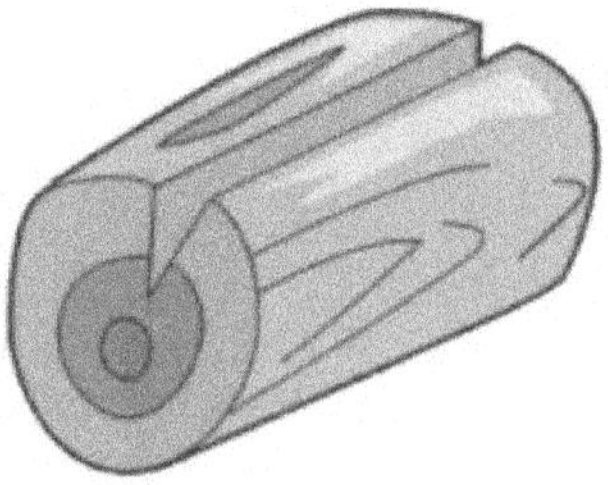

The dog is thrilled.

The hog is big.

She is jogging.

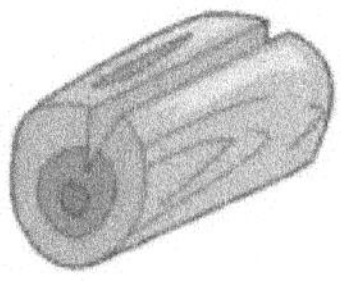

The log is small.

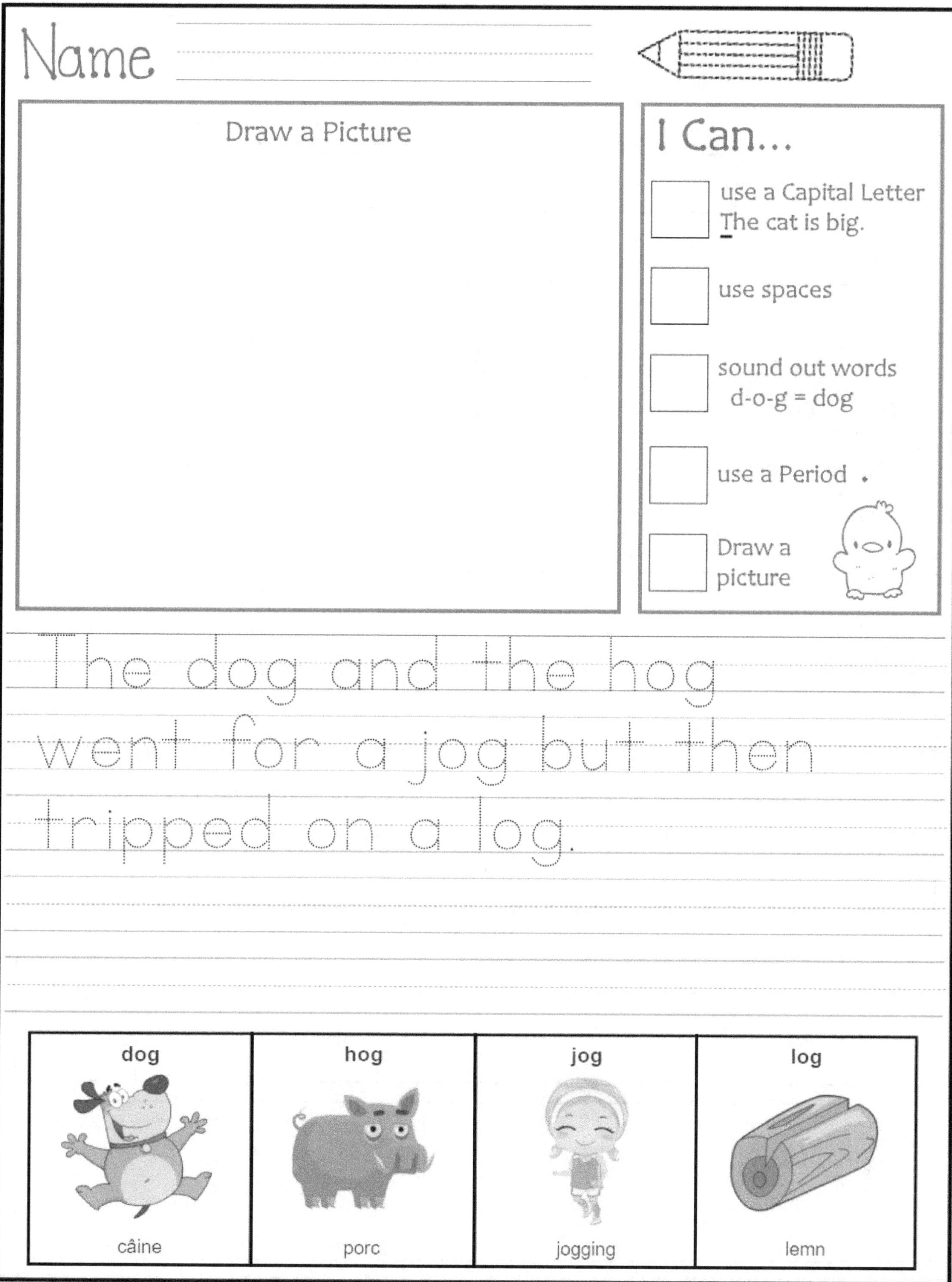

Name

Draw a Picture

I Can...

use a Capital Letter
The cat is big.

use spaces

sound out words
d-o-g = dog

use a Period .

Draw a
picture

The dog and the hog went for a jog but then tripped on a log.

dog
câine

hog
porc

jog
jogging

log
lemn

Name: ____________________ Date: ____________________

Today is: Monday | Tuesday | Wednesday | Thursday | Friday

Direction: Trace and read the sentences.

bug	hug	jug	mug
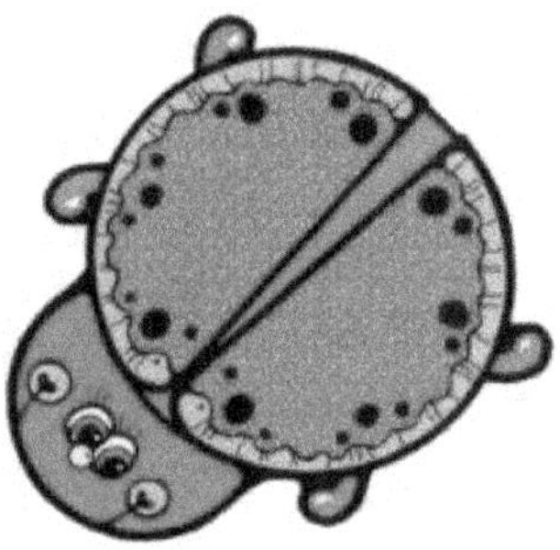			
gândac	îmbrăţişare	ulcior	halbă

The bug is colorful.

She is hugging.

The jug has milk in it.

He has a mug.

Name

Draw a Picture

I Can...

use a Capital Letter
The cat is big.

use spaces

sound out words
d-o-g = dog

use a Period .

Draw a
picture

The bug hugged the jug
and the mug which was
full of jam.

bug
gândac

hug
îmbrăţişare

jug
ulcior

mug
halbă

Name: ______________________ Date: ______________________

Today is: Monday Tuesday Wednesday Thursday Friday

Direction: Trace and read the sentences.

cot	dot	hot	pot

pat	punct	fierbinte	oală

This is my cot.

There are many dots.

It is very hot.

He has a plant pot.

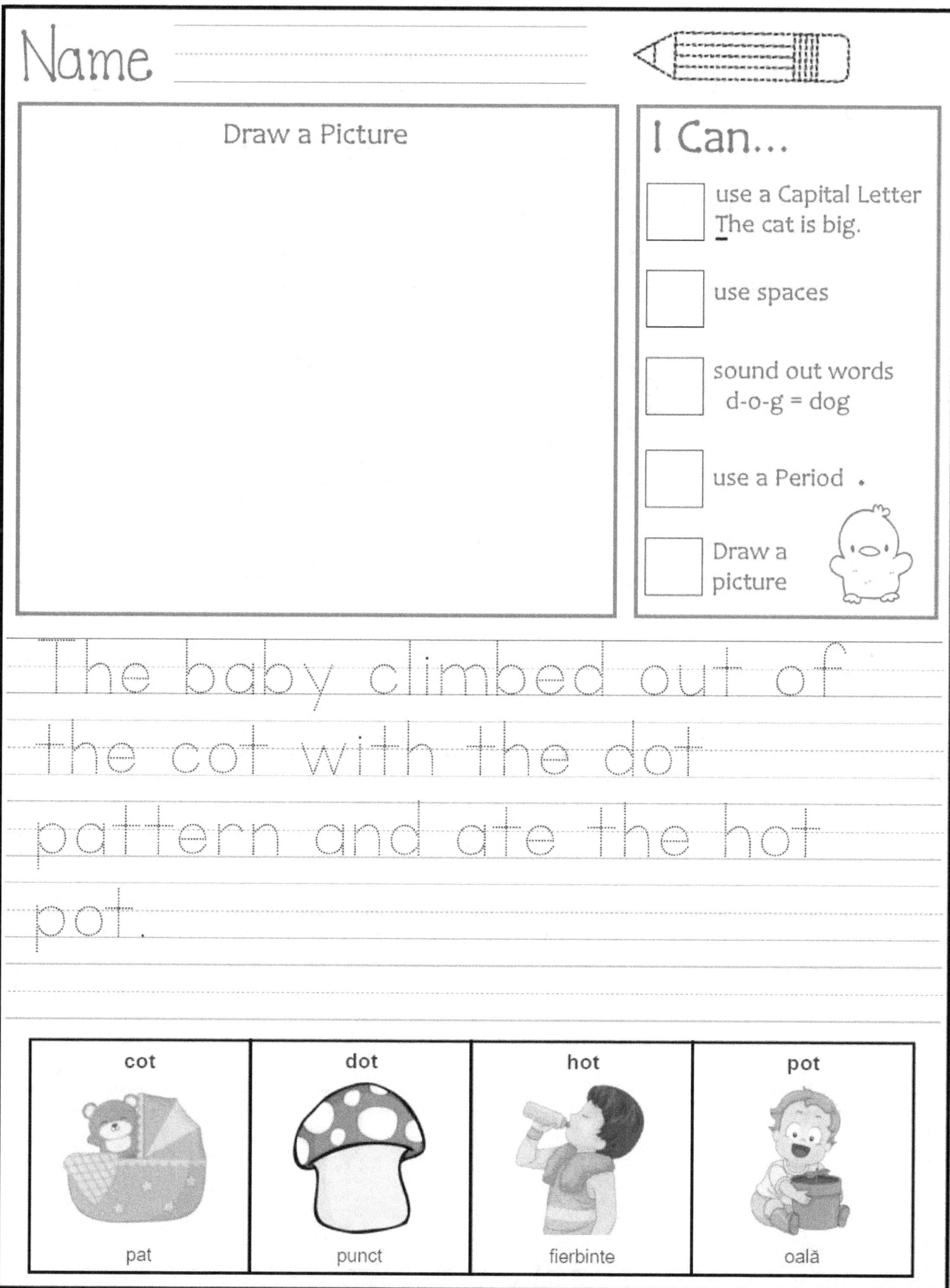

Name

Draw a Picture

I Can...

- [ ] use a Capital Letter
  The cat is big.
- [ ] use spaces
- [ ] sound out words
  d-o-g = dog
- [ ] use a Period .
- [ ] Draw a picture

The baby climbed out of the cot with the dot pattern and ate the hot pot.

cot	dot	hot	pot
pat	punct	fierbinte	oală

Name: _________________________ Date: _______________

Today is: Monday   Tuesday   Wednesday   Thursday   Friday

Direction: Read the words and make a sentence.

fun	gun	run	sun
distracţie	armă	alerga	soare

Name ___________________________________

<table>
<tr><td>

Draw a Picture

</td><td>

I Can...

☐ use a Capital Letter
  The cat is big.

☐ use spaces

☐ sound out words
   d-o-g = dog

☐ use a Period .

☐ Draw a
  picture

</td></tr>
</table>

Name: _______________________ Date: _______________________

Today is: Monday Tuesday Wednesday Thursday Friday

Name: _________________________ Date: _______________

Today is: | Monday | Tuesday | Wednesday |
| Thursday | Friday |

Direction: Read the words and make a sentence.

bag	**rag**	**tag**	**wag**
sac	cârpă	etichetă	datul

Draw a Picture

I Can...

- [ ] use a Capital Letter
  The cat is big.

- [ ] use spaces

- [ ] sound out words
  d-o-g = dog

- [ ] use a Period .

- [ ] Draw a picture

Name: _____________________ Date: _____________________

Today is: Monday Tuesday Wednesday Thursday Friday

Name: _________________________ Date: _______________

Today is: [Monday] [Tuesday] [Wednesday]
[Thursday] [Friday]

Direction: Read the words and make a sentence.

can	**man**	**pan**	**van**
o cutie	om	tigaie	dubă

Name

Draw a Picture

I Can...

- [ ] use a Capital Letter
  The cat is big.

- [ ] use spaces

- [ ] sound out words
  d-o-g = dog

- [ ] use a Period .

- [ ] Draw a picture

Name: _______________________   Date: _______________

Today is: [Monday] [Tuesday] [Wednesday] [Thursday] [Friday]

Name: _______________________ Date: _______________

Today is: Monday | Tuesday | Wednesday
Thursday | Friday

Direction: Read the words and make a sentence.

cut	**gut**	**hut**	**nut**
tăia	intestin	colibă	nuca

Name

Draw a Picture

I Can...

☐ use a Capital Letter
The cat is big.

☐ use spaces

☐ sound out words
d-o-g = dog

☐ use a Period .

☐ Draw a picture

Name: _______________ Date: _______________

Today is: Monday Tuesday Wednesday

Thursday Friday

Name: _________________ Date: _________________

Today is: | Monday | Tuesday | Wednesday |
| Thursday | Friday |

Direction: Read the words and make a sentence.

| **fat** | **cat** | **hat** | **mat** |
| gras | pisică | pălărie | mat |

Name _______________________

Draw a Picture

I Can...

- [ ] use a Capital Letter
  The cat is big.

- [ ] use spaces

- [ ] sound out words
  d-o-g = dog

- [ ] use a Period .

- [ ] Draw a picture

Name: ___________________ Date: ___________________

Today is: Monday Tuesday Wednesday Thursday Friday

Name: _________________________ Date: _______________

Today is: [Monday] [Tuesday] [Wednesday]
[Thursday] [Friday]

Direction: Read the words and make a sentence.

cab	lab	tab	crab
taxi	laborator	fila	crab

Name

Draw a Picture

I Can...

- [ ] use a Capital Letter
  The cat is big.

- [ ] use spaces

- [ ] sound out words
  d-o-g = dog

- [ ] use a Period .

- [ ] Draw a picture

Name: _______________________ Date: _______________

Today is: Monday | Tuesday | Wednesday
Thursday | Friday

Name: _______________ Date: _______________

Today is: Monday Tuesday Wednesday
Thursday Friday

Direction: Read the words and make a sentence.

ham	**jam**	**ram**	**clam**
șuncă	gem	oaie	coajă

Name

Draw a Picture

I Can...

- [ ] use a Capital Letter
  <u>T</u>he cat is big.

- [ ] use spaces

- [ ] sound out words
  d-o-g = dog

- [ ] use a Period .

- [ ] Draw a picture

Name: _______________________ Date: _______________________

Today is: Monday Tuesday Wednesday Thursday Friday

bed	led	red	wed
pat	conducere	roșu	nuntă

Name

Draw a Picture

I Can...

- [ ] use a Capital Letter
  The cat is big.

- [ ] use spaces

- [ ] sound out words
  d-o-g = dog

- [ ] use a Period .

- [ ] Draw a
  picture

Name: _______________________ Date: _______________

Today is: Monday   Tuesday   Wednesday
          Thursday   Friday

Name: _______________ Date: _______________

Today is: Monday | Tuesday | Wednesday

Thursday | Friday

Direction: Read the words and make a sentence.

bad	**dad**	**mad**	**sad**
rău	tata	nebun	trist

Name

Draw a Picture

I Can...

- [ ] use a Capital Letter
  <u>T</u>he cat is big.

- [ ] use spaces

- [ ] sound out words
  d-o-g = dog

- [ ] use a Period .

- [ ] Draw a picture

Name: _______________________   Date: _______________________

Today is: Monday Tuesday Wednesday Thursday Friday

Name: _________________________ Date: _____________

Today is: Monday Tuesday Wednesday

Thursday Friday

Direction: Read the words and make a sentence.

den	**hen**	**pen**	**ten**
bârlog	găină	grajduri	zece

Draw a Picture

I Can...

- [ ] use a Capital Letter
  The cat is big.
- [ ] use spaces
- [ ] sound out words
  d-o-g = dog
- [ ] use a Period .
- [ ] Draw a picture

Name: _________________________   Date: _________________

Today is: [Monday] [Tuesday] [Wednesday]
          [Thursday] [Friday]

Name: _______________________ Date: _______________________

Today is: Monday   Tuesday   Wednesday

Thursday   Friday

Direction: Read the words and make a sentence.

gum	mum	sum	drum
cleios	mămică	sumă	tobă

Name ______________________________

<table>
<tr><td>

Draw a Picture

</td><td>

I Can...

☐ use a Capital Letter
The cat is big.

☐ use spaces

☐ sound out words
d-o-g = dog

☐ use a Period .

☐ Draw a picture

</td></tr>
</table>

Name: _______________________   Date: _______________

Today is: Monday Tuesday Wednesday Thursday Friday

Name: _________________ Date: _____________

Today is: [Monday] [Tuesday] [Wednesday]
[Thursday] [Friday]

Direction: Read the words and make a sentence.

bid	**hid**	**kid**	**lid**
ofertă	ascunde	copil	capac

Name

Draw a Picture

I Can...

☐ use a Capital Letter
The cat is big.

☐ use spaces

☐ sound out words
d-o-g = dog

☐ use a Period .

☐ Draw a picture

Name: _______________________ Date: _______________

Today is: Monday Tuesday Wednesday Thursday Friday

Name: ___________________ Date: ___________________

Today is: Monday Tuesday Wednesday Thursday Friday

Direction: Read the words and make a sentence.

big	**dig**	**pig**	**wig**
mare	săpa	porc	perucă

Name ______________________________

<table>
<tr><td>Draw a Picture</td><td>I Can...</td></tr>
</table>

I Can...

- [ ] use a Capital Letter
  The cat is big.
- [ ] use spaces
- [ ] sound out words
  d-o-g = dog
- [ ] use a Period .
- [ ] Draw a picture

Name: _______________________ Date: _______________

Today is: Monday Tuesday Wednesday Thursday Friday

Name: _______________ Date: _______________

Today is: Monday Tuesday Wednesday Thursday Friday

Direction: Read the words and make a sentence.

bin	fin	pin	win
cos	aripioară	bolț	victorie

Draw a Picture

I Can...

use a Capital Letter
The cat is big.

use spaces

sound out words
d-o-g = dog

use a Period .

Draw a
picture

Name: _________________________   Date: _________________

Today is: | Monday | Tuesday | Wednesday |
          | Thursday | Friday |

Name: _______________________ Date: _______________________

Today is: Monday Tuesday Wednesday Thursday Friday

Direction: Read the words and make a sentence.

hip	lip	nip	sip
şold	buze	muşcătură	băutură

Name ___________________

Draw a Picture

I Can...

- [ ] use a Capital Letter
  The cat is big.

- [ ] use spaces

- [ ] sound out words
  d-o-g = dog

- [ ] use a Period .

- [ ] Draw a picture

Name: _______________________   Date: _______________________

Today is: Monday   Tuesday   Wednesday   Thursday   Friday

Name: _________________________ Date: _________________________

Today is: [Monday] [Tuesday] [Wednesday] [Thursday] [Friday]

Direction: Read the words and make a sentence.

fit	**hit**	**kit**	**sit**
potrivi	lovit	trusă	sta

Name

Draw a Picture

I Can...

- [ ] use a Capital Letter
  The cat is big.

- [ ] use spaces

- [ ] sound out words
  d-o-g = dog

- [ ] use a Period .

- [ ] Draw a picture

Name: _______________________ Date: _______________

Today is: Monday | Tuesday | Wednesday
Thursday | Friday

Name: _________________ Date: _______________

Today is: Monday Tuesday Wednesday
Thursday Friday

Direction: Read the words and make a sentence.

cob	job	rob	sob
porumb	datorie	jefui	strigăt

Name _______________

<table>
<tr><td>Draw a Picture</td><td>I Can...</td></tr>
</table>

Draw a Picture

I Can...

- [ ] use a Capital Letter
  The cat is big.

- [ ] use spaces

- [ ] sound out words
  d-o-g = dog

- [ ] use a Period .

- [ ] Draw a picture

Name: _______________________   Date: _______________

Today is: Monday Tuesday Wednesday Thursday Friday

Name: ___________________ Date: _______________

Today is: Monday Tuesday Wednesday
Thursday Friday

Direction: Read the words and make a sentence.

dog	hog	jog	log
câine	porc	jogging	lemn

Name ___________________________

<table>
<tr><td>

Draw a Picture

</td><td>

I Can...

☐ use a Capital Letter
The cat is big.

☐ use spaces

☐ sound out words
d-o-g = dog

☐ use a Period .

☐ Draw a
picture

</td></tr>
</table>

Name: _______________________ Date: _______________

Today is: Monday Tuesday Wednesday Thursday Friday

Name: __________________ Date: __________

Today is: Monday Tuesday Wednesday
Thursday Friday

Direction: Read the words and make a sentence.

bug	**hug**	**jug**	**mug**
gândac	îmbrăţişare	ulcior	halbă

Name

Draw a Picture

I Can...

- [ ] use a Capital Letter
  <u>T</u>he cat is big.

- [ ] use spaces

- [ ] sound out words
  d-o-g = dog

- [ ] use a Period .

- [ ] Draw a picture

Name: _______________________ Date: _______________

Today is: Monday Tuesday Wednesday Thursday Friday

Name: _______________________ Date: _______________

Today is: [Monday] [Tuesday] [Wednesday]
[Thursday] [Friday]

Direction: Read the words and make a sentence.

cot	**dot**	**hot**	**pot**
pat	punct	fierbinte	oală

Name

Draw a Picture

I Can...

- [ ] use a Capital Letter
  The cat is big.

- [ ] use spaces

- [ ] sound out words
  d-o-g = dog

- [ ] use a Period .

- [ ] Draw a picture

Name: _______________________   Date: _______________________

Today is: Monday Tuesday Wednesday Thursday Friday